Table of Contents

M000034415

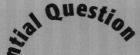

Essential Question

Where do scientific discoveries lead us?

The Power of Electricity

Benchmark
EDUCATION

The Power of Electricity

Student Objectives

I will be able to:

- Read and analyze informational and literary texts about economic resources.

- Share ideas with my peers.

- Build my vocabulary knowledge.

- Conduct research to write an opinion essay.

Tips for Text Annotation

As you read closely for different purposes, remember to annotate the text. Use the symbols below. Add new symbols in the spaces provided.

Symbol	Purpose
<u>underline</u>	Identify a key detail.
☆	Star an important idea in the margin.
① ② ③	Mark a sequence of events.
(magma)	Circle a key word or phrase.
?	Mark a question you have about information in the text. Write your question in the margin.
!	Indicate an idea in the text you find interesting. Comment on this idea in the margin.

Your annotations might look like this.

Notes	**The Gold Rush**
	16 The migration on the Oregon Trail became an annual event. ① Thousands of emigrants began to join the wagon trains heading West. ② Then in ☆ 1848, gold was discovered in California. The (lure) of rich farmlands now changed to fields of gold. ③ By 1850, more than fifty thousand people traveled the Oregon Trail West. Instead of turning toward Oregon near the end of the trail, many turned to California. They hoped to find their fortune mining or panning for gold instead of farming.
That's a lot of people!	
Who was the first person to discover gold?	

Credits
Editor: Joanne Tangorra
Contributing Editors: Jeffrey B. Fuerst, Brett Kelly
Creative Director: Laurie Berger
Art Directors: Melody DeJesus, Kathryn DelVecchio-Kempa, Doug McGredy, Chris Moroch
Production: Kosta Triantafillis
Director of Photography: Doug Schneider
Photo Assistant: Jackie Friedman

Photo credits: Table of Contents A: Bloomberg/Contributor/Getty Images; Pages 3B, 19: Detlev van Ravenswaay/Science Source; Page 4B: Mail Today/Getty Images; Page 5: © Bikas Das/AP/Corbis; Page 7: Artist's impression of the Benjamin Franklin's/Universal History Archive/UIG/Bridgeman Images; Page 15B: © Heritage Images/Corbis; Page 15C: © GL Archive/Alamy; Page 15D: © David Cole/Alamy; Pages 15E, 25A, 26B: The Granger Collection, NYC; Page 18A: © Jessica Hill/AP/Corbis; Page 18B: © Bettmann/Corbis; Page 22: © nobleIMAGES/Alamy; Page 23B: © Niday Picture Library/Alamy; Page 27: Science Source

Permissions: "Power Restored in India" from *TIME for Kids*, August 1, 2012. © 2012 Time Inc. All rights reserved. Used by permission and protected by the Copyright Laws of the United States. The printing, copying, redistribution, or retransmission of this content without express written permission is prohibited.

LEXILE® is a trademark of MetaMetrics, Inc., and is registered in the United States and abroad.

E-book and digital teacher's guide available at benchmarkuniverse.com.

BENCHMARK EDUCATION COMPANY
145 Huguenot Street • New Rochelle, NY • 10801

Toll-Free 1-877-236-2465
www.benchmarkeducation.com
www.benchmarkuniverse.com

3

Remember to annotate as you read.

Notes

August 1, 2012

Power Restored in India

by Abby Lieberman

Power is back up and running after massive blackouts leave millions in the dark.

1   After experiencing the largest power blackout in history, people in India can finally turn on the lights. On July 30, India's northern electric grid failed. It left 370 million people without power. By the next day, that number had grown to 620 million. The electrical blackout had spread to more than half the country. The specific cause of the outages is unknown. As of August 1, power had been restored throughout India.

2   The blackout stranded passengers at railway stations. In factories and offices, work ground to a halt. Miners were trapped in a coal mine in West Bengal. In New Delhi, India's capital, traffic snarled when traffic lights stopped working.

During the blackout in New Delhi, trains stopped running.

What Happened?

3   The failure of three national power grids plunged half the country into darkness. An electric grid is a network of power stations, fuel, and power lines that work together to deliver electricity. A failure in any part of the network can cause the power to go out.

4   The exact cause of the grid failures is unknown. Officials believe that the outage was due to areas consuming too much energy, as India's power division struggled to meet the increasing demand for energy. The grids were unable to produce the amount of energy that residents were using. "If they overdraw, this is the result," said India's power minister, Veerappa Moily.

5   India is the world's second-most populous nation. It is also a growing economic force. Power shortages are not uncommon in the country. Now, many are wondering whether the country needs to work harder to improve its infrastructure, or basic facilities. According to the Associated Press, Moily said that the government would not allow a massive blackout to happen again.

A barber cuts his customer's hair by candlelight.

Notes

Benjamin Franklin: The Dawn of Electrical Technology

by Laura McDonald

1   Benjamin Franklin was one of the most influential thinkers of the eighteenth century. He was one of our country's founding fathers, who helped to draft the Declaration of Independence and the United States Constitution. But he also was an inventor and scientist. He made some of the most important contributions to the history of science.

2   One of Franklin's ideas changed the course of scientific history. One stormy day in June 1752, Franklin stood in the doorway of a shed with his son William. They were flying a kite. Franklin wanted to show that lightning was a type of electric current.

3   Many people at the time believed lightning was a form of magic. But Franklin's observations had led him to conclude that lightning was a natural form of electricity. He learned through his work and the work of other scientists that electric energy was conducted through metal. So, he wanted to find out if lightning would pass through a metal object. To do this, Franklin tied a metal key to a kite and went out to test his hypothesis.

A Man of Science and Letters

4   An account of this famous event was written by scientist Joseph Priestley many years later:

5   "The kite being raised . . . he observed some loose threads of the hempen string to stand erect, and to avoid one another, just as if they had been suspended on a common conductor . . . he immediately presented his knuckle to the key, and . . .he perceived a very evident electric spark ...."

6   Franklin collected "electric fire" in a Leyden (LY-den) jar. A Leyden jar is a glass jar with a glass layer sandwiched between two metal layers. Electrons build up on the metal layers. When a conductor connects the two metal layers, the jar produces an electric spark. Franklin used a Leyden jar to conduct experiments with lightning. He proved that it was a form of electricity.

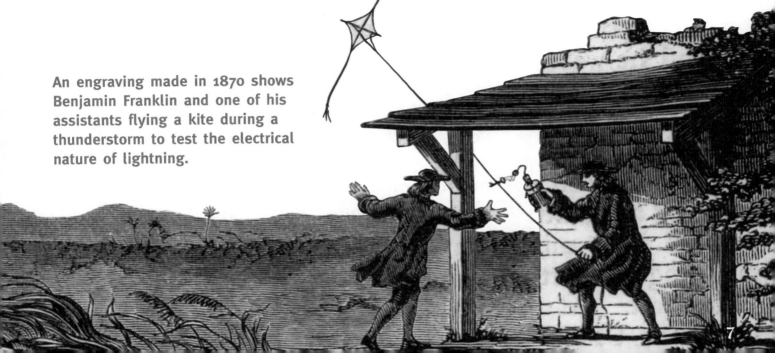

An engraving made in 1870 shows Benjamin Franklin and one of his assistants flying a kite during a thunderstorm to test the electrical nature of lightning.

600 B.C.E.
Thales of Miletus describes how amber can become charged by rubbing —what we now call static electricity.

1600 C.E.
William Gilbert coins term *electricity,* which comes from Greek word for amber.

1751
Franklin's letters are published as *Experiments and Observations on Electricity.*

1752
Franklin conducts kite experiment, invents lightning rod, and proves lightning has electrical charges.

1767
Joseph Priestley finds that electricity follows Newton's law of gravity.

1800
First electric battery invented by Alessandro Volta.

Notes

7   Franklin also shared his work and techniques with others. He wrote to scientist Peter Collinson to tell him how to build a kite and draw "electric fire" from lightning.:

8   . . . *As soon as any of the thunder clouds come over the kite, the pointed wire will draw the electric fire from them . . . and from electric fire thus obtained, spirits may be kindled, and all the other electric experiments be performed, which are usually done by the help of a rubbed glass globe or tube, and thereby the sameness of the electric matter with that of lightning completely demonstrated.*

"Would not these pointed Rods probably draw the Electrical Fire silently out of a Cloud before it came nigh enough to strike, and thereby secure us from that most sudden and terrible Mischief!"
—BEN FRANKLIN, 1750

9   Franklin went on to make other important inventions and discoveries. By connecting Leyden jars together, he invented an early type of battery. Franklin also invented the lightning rod.

10   Franklin's studies of lightning helped people understand electricity. Lightning rods have saved many people's homes and lives. Franklin also coined many of the words we still use to describe electricity. Battery, charge, and conductor are just some of the terms Franklin invented.

11   Franklin was a curious and intelligent man. He helped to form the first public library and the first fire department in Pennsylvania. Franklin also helped to write the Declaration of Independence and the U.S. Constitution. Franklin accomplished many great things. But he was most famous around the world as the man who discovered the nature of lightning.

When lightning strikes a building, it is conducted through the lightning rod harmlessly into the ground.

Word Study Read

Remember to annotate as you read.

Notes

Blackout, 1965

1   When the power went out during my last stay at Granddad's, I was miserable. After all, my cell phone needed charging, I was missing my favorite television programs, and Granddad's apartment was stifling without air conditioning. "How long is this blackout going to last?" I whined.

2   Granddad handed me a flashlight and gave me a playful nudge. "Aw, it's not so bad," he said. "You should have been in New York City in 1965. Now that was a *real* blackout!

3   "Of course, the elevators in my office building weren't working," Granddad said, "so my coworkers and I inched our way down sixteen flights of stairs using candles. The subways were out, too, so we ate in a restaurant by candlelight and then snagged places to sleep in a hotel lobby. The next day I found out that some people had been stuck in subway cars. Others had been trapped in elevators in the Empire State Building! Ordinary citizens were in the streets directing traffic and drivers were obeying! Yet people didn't panic. They just tried to help one another."

4   "Well, maybe this blackout isn't so bad," I said. "At least we're not stuck in an elevator!" Just as I spoke, the lights flickered on and the air conditioner resumed its familiar humming.

5   Granddad grabbed the remote control and plopped down in his recliner chair. "Yeah, life can be exciting during a blackout," he chuckled, "but it's a lot easier with electricity."

BuildReflectWrite

Build Knowledge

Identify Benjamin Franklin's most important discoveries and inventions, and their effects on people's lives. Then explain which one you think has most affected our modern lives today.

Ben Franklin's Discoveries/Inventions	Effects on People's Lives

Ben Franklin's most important discovery/invention in today's world:

Reflect

Where do scientific discoveries lead us?

Based on this week's texts, write down new ideas and questions you have about the essential question.

_____

_____

_____

_____

_____

_____

_____

Research and Writing

Opinion

Research one invention or discovery that has affected the way we power our lives. In an opinion essay, explain why you think this invention or discovery has had the greatest impact on the way we use electricity. Make sure to defend your opinion with reasons and evidence.

Choose Your Topic

Conduct a pre-search to identify an invention or discovery you would like to research. Construct three or more guiding questions that will help you focus your research on the information you will need to write your opinion essay.

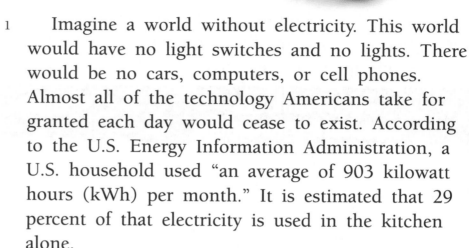

Remember to annotate as you read.

The Power of Electricity

by Kathy Furgang

1   Imagine a world without electricity. This world would have no light switches and no lights. There would be no cars, computers, or cell phones. Almost all of the technology Americans take for granted each day would cease to exist. According to the U.S. Energy Information Administration, a U.S. household used "an average of 903 kilowatt hours (kWh) per month." It is estimated that 29 percent of that electricity is used in the kitchen alone.

2   In today's world, most people depend on electricity and technology to live and work. People rely on electricity for light and heat. They need it to cook and clean. They use it to prepare and preserve food. They use it to travel from place to place. They use it to communicate. They even rely on electricity for entertainment.

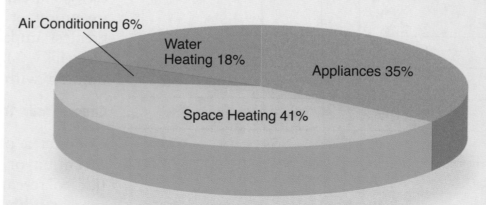

U.S. Household Electricity Consumption

Air Conditioning 6%
Water Heating 18%
Appliances 35%
Space Heating 41%

Source: U.S. Energy Information Administration, Residential Energy Consumption Survey 2011–2012 (based on 2009 usage)

Electrons on the Move

3   But what is electricity? Most people think of it as the "power" that they use to run all of their appliances. But what causes this "power"? The answer is in the science of atoms.

4   All matter—everything in the universe—is made of tiny building blocks called atoms. And all atoms are made up of particles. Positively charged particles are called protons. Particles with no charge are called neutrons. Negatively charged particles are called electrons. Protons and neutrons are packed tightly in the nucleus, or center, of each atom. Electrons orbit around the nucleus. Sometimes electrons get loose and move to the orbit of another atom. Electricity is the movement, or flow, of electrons from atom to atom.

5   There are two types of electricity. When the electric charge is stationary, or not moving, the result is static electricity. For example, if a person's clothes were to rub against a blanket, they would generate friction. This friction would cause electrons from the blanket to move to the clothing. The result would give the clothing a negatively charged static electricity.

Fast Fact
Humans make electricity inside their bodies, too. Every thought or action the body makes is caused by electrical signals from the brain to the cells.

Electric Currents

6   When an electric charge is moving through matter, the result is current electricity.

7   Materials that have a loose hold on their electrons are called conductors. Electrons move through the material easily. A continuous flow of electrons is an electric current.

8   There are two types of currents. When the electrons always flow in the same direction, it is called direct current, or DC. Flashlights and cell phones all use batteries and DC power. A battery has two terminals, one positive and one negative. Electrons flow in the same direction between the two terminals. An alternating current, or AC, reverses, or alternates, direction fifty or sixty times per second. Everything that plugs into an outlet uses AC power. Alternating current is used when high-power voltages are required.

9   Over time, scientists have learned to harness the flow of energy. They have learned how to transfer, convert, and store this energy. These advances in electrical technology have made it possible to power the modern world.

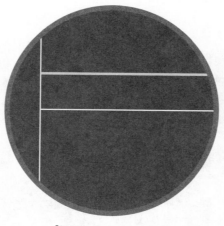

direct current

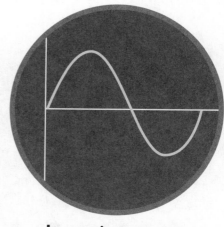

alternating current

Pioneers of Electricity

The technologies people use to power their lives were made possible by a series of discoveries and inventions. Each of the key players in electricity added his own spark of genius.

1752 Benjamin Franklin

Lightning in a Bottle
Franklin proved that lightning is a type of electricity, storing it in Leyden jars. In his footsteps, many scientists continued to explore different ways to produce and use electricity efficiently.

1800 Alessandro Volta

The First Battery
Volta placed large plates made of different types of metals into a chemical solution. The combination sent electricity flowing through a wire. He called his invention a voltaic pile.

1831 Michael Faraday

Electric Generator
Faraday found a way to move electrons through a wire without using chemicals. He set electrons free by rotating a copper disc between two magnets, sending electricity flowing through a wire via electromagnetism.

1879 Thomas Edison

Electric Lighting System
Edison created a complete electric lighting system, with generators, power lines, light fixtures, and the first electric lightbulb.

1887 Nikola Tesla

The Induction Motor
Tesla's induction motor generated alternating current (AC). Tesla's technology outmatched Edison's direct current (DC) system. AC still powers the electric grid we use today!

Generating Electricity

10   Where does the electricity that people consume come from? Energy can be converted, or changed, from one form to another. That means stored or mechanical energy can be converted to electric energy.

11   According to the U.S. Department of Energy, most power plants in the United States use heat energy to generate electricity. They use the heat that is released from burning fossil fuels (coal, natural gas, or oil) to boil water into steam. The pressure of the steam turns the blades of a turbine. The spinning turbine powers a generator that releases electric energy. Some generators convert nuclear power into electricity. Other generators convert wind or solar energy into electricity. This electricity is transmitted along wires to customers.

12   In the United States, electricity starts at power plants and enters a complex power grid. This grid can be compared to a network of roads. Highways are like the main power lines that come from the power plants. Traffic usually flows fast along the highways until it gets close to major cities. The flow of electricity in the power lines works the same way. As it gets close to its destination, electricity has to be directed.

13   Control centers throughout the electric grid direct power through electric substations. These control centers act like traffic cops, making sure the electricity goes where it is needed. Eventually, electricity makes its way through the network of power lines to its destination—the outlets in homes and businesses. Most of the work to control the flow of electricity is done automatically by computers. This is where trouble can begin.

Blackouts

14   When a computer malfunctions, or breaks, transmission is obstructed, or blocked. The result is a blackout, where the electric power fails in a region. Most of the time, only a small area is affected by a blackout. However, sometimes the effects are catastrophic.

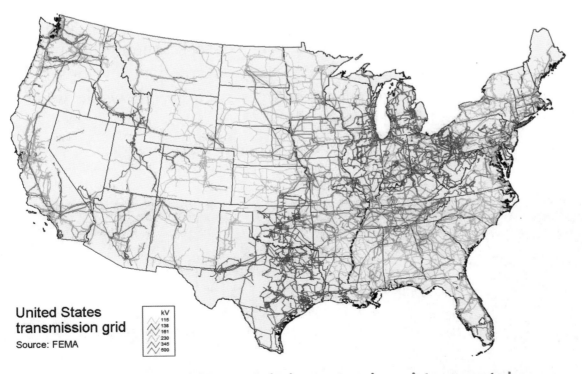

United States transmission grid
Source: FEMA

| kV |
| 115 |
| 138 |
| 161 |
| 230 |
| 345 |
| 500 |

The U.S. electricity transmission system is an interconnected network of more than 150,000 miles of high-voltage power lines.

15   In 1965, a massive blackout hit the Northeast. It left thirty million people in the dark. The problem was caused by one faulty transmission line. When it stopped working, the electricity overloaded power lines and shut them down. This caused a domino effect throughout a large area. Like falling dominoes, the power lines shut down one after the other.

16   Engineers have improved the power system over the last fifty years, but as the demand for electricity continues to grow, region-wide power failures and blackouts have occurred. Improvements are needed to make sure the lights stay on, but people have different opinions about what these improvements should be.

Conserving Energy for the Future

17   Many people think better technologies are needed to provide electricity. More efficient technologies would help conserve energy resources by reducing waste. Scientists are also developing alternative energy sources such as renewable wind and solar power.

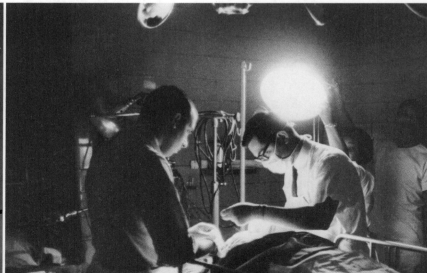

18   The National Aeronautics and Space Administration (NASA) has plans to launch a series of mirrors into space to collect energy from the sun and redirect it to Earth. In the future, NASA may also use kites to capture the wind's energy at high altitudes, far from Earth's surface.

19   Others feel that nonelectric technology is a better answer. Engineer and inventor Yasuyuki Fujimura hopes people will soon avoid the use of electricity. He uses his education in physics to develop new hi-tech nonelectric appliances. Fujimura explains, "There are many interesting home appliances that can be operated without electric power. One example is a nonelectric refrigerator. It uses a phenomenon called radiational cooling together with the natural convection currents of water." Fujimura hopes his inventions will promote a nonelectric lifestyle.

20   Until nonelectric appliances like Fujimura's designs are in every household, the world will continue to rely on electricity. This demand for power will force scientists to improve the technologies that deliver electricity.

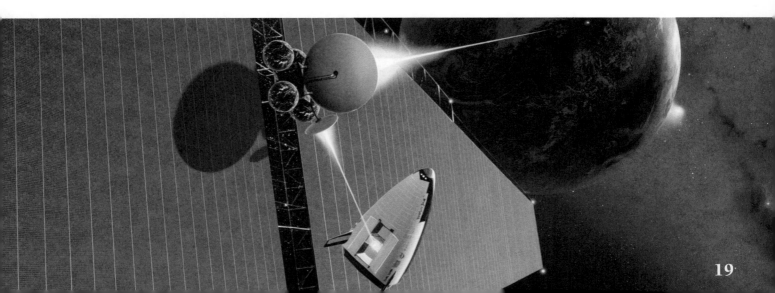

Hoover Dam

1   Electricity is essential to our lives. We use it to charge our phones, operate our kitchen appliances, and light our streets. Where does all this electricity come from? Much of it comes from power plants that run on fossil or nuclear fuel. Some is generated by solar or wind power. And some of it comes from hydroelectric plants that harness the power of water. One of the largest hydroelectric plants in the country is housed at the base of Hoover Dam.

2   Built in the 1930s, Hoover Dam is a huge concrete structure that spans the Colorado River between Arizona and Nevada. The dam was built to control the flow of the river and provide water to the barren desert. It was also built to produce electricity. When the Colorado River was dammed, a lake called Lake Mead was created. The water from Lake Mead is used to generate electricity. As the water from the lake travels down large pipes alongside Hoover Dam, it spins turbines at the base of the dam. The turbines then turn generators that produce electricity. Where does electricity from Hoover Dam go? Much of it goes to metropolitan areas in Southern California. It also goes to parts of Arizona and Nevada.

3   Although the production of electricity at Hoover Dam doesn't create toxic chemical pollution, the creation of dams can be controversial today. Many people feel that dams and the lakes they create have a harmful ecological effect. Still, dams are an important source of electric power. And Hoover Dam is one of the greatest American dams ever built.

BuildReflectWrite

Build Knowledge

Jot down your ideas about the meaning of the word *electricity*.

Electricity	
1) Based on the reading, "The Power of Electricity," what does the word *electricity* mean?	**2) What context clues help the reader determine the meaning of the word?**
3) How is the word *electricity* used in the reading? Give a few examples.	**4) How did the context of the reading help you determine the meaning of the word?**

Reflect

Where do scientific discoveries lead us?

Based on this week's texts, write down new ideas and questions you have about the essential question.

_____

_____

_____

_____

_____

_____

_____

Research and Writing

Opinion

Research one invention or discovery that has affected the way we power our lives. In an opinion essay, explain why you think this invention or discovery has had the greatest impact on the way we use electricity. Make sure to defend your opinion with reasons and evidence.

Conduct Research

Use your guiding questions to conduct research this week. Gather information from at least three sources, including both print and online sources. Use your sources to plan your opinion essay.

Remember to annotate as you read.

Notes

Nikola Tesla:
Electrifying Inventor

by Alexandra Hanson-Harding

1   Nikola Tesla was a visionary and one of the most brilliant scientists who ever lived. As B.A. Behrend, vice president of the Institute of Electrical Engineers, said at that group's meeting in 1917: "Were we to seize and eliminate from our industrial world the result of Mr. Tesla's work, the wheels of industry would cease to turn, our electric cars and trains would stop, our towns would be dark and our mills would be idle and dead. His name marks an epoch in the advance of electrical science."

2   Scientists call Tesla "the father of the electric age" for his revolutionary inventions. His ideas brought about major change. Yet his work has been left off the pages of most history books.

Chicago lit up at night

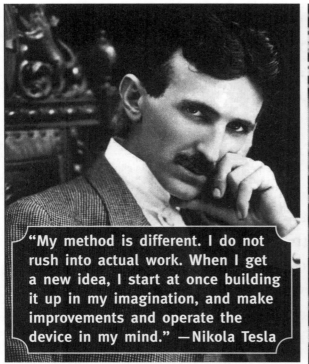

"My method is different. I do not rush into actual work. When I get a new idea, I start at once building it up in my imagination, and make improvements and operate the device in my mind." —Nikola Tesla

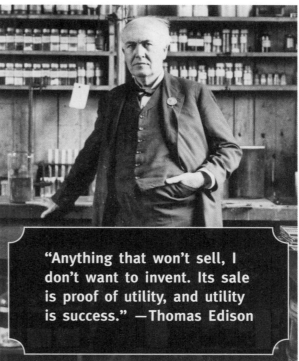

"Anything that won't sell, I don't want to invent. Its sale is proof of utility, and utility is success." —Thomas Edison

3   One reason for this was because Tesla competed throughout his career with fellow inventor Thomas Edison. The two were as different as night and day. Edison was a businessman first and foremost. He was always thinking of ways to make money from his inventions. Tesla, on the other hand, was devoted to science—not money. He valued what his inventions could do for the world, not his bank account. When Tesla did earn money from his inventions, he spent his profits on more experiments and a luxurious lifestyle.

4   Edison's ideas were practical—simple and useful but not always the most efficient or advanced. Tesla's vision was more ambitious. Some of his ideas seemed far-fetched, such as a particle gun powerful enough to end all wars. Others, such as AC current, completely changed the way the world works.

Notes

5   Tesla was also a visionary whose inventions led to such common items as radios, robots, remote controls, spark plugs, fluorescent lights, and huge machines that shot lightning bolts. More importantly, he developed the system of delivering

This is Tesla demonstrating a radio-controlled boat in 1898.

electric currents for energy that we use today. He made advances in many different fields, including engineering, robotics, X-ray technology, electricity, and magnetism. He had hundreds of patents to his name—and he was generous about sharing them. Unlike Edison, Tesla had no head for business and often made poor business decisions.

6   For example, when the Italian inventor Guglielmo Marconi successfully put in a patent for a radio several years after Tesla did, using many ideas very similar to his, Tesla just laughed it off. "Marconi is a good fellow. Let him continue. He is using seventeen of my patents," he said. Meanwhile, Marconi made a fortune with his radio, and Tesla made nothing from his.

"I don't care that they stole my idea . . . I care that they don't have any of their own."
—Nikola Tesla

Meet Nikola Tesla

7   Tesla was born in what is now Croatia to Serbian parents in 1856. His intelligence was clear from a young age as he quickly was able to memorize entire books. Tesla most likely got his love of inventing things from his mother, who invented household items. He studied at various universities, but was a late bloomer. He did not focus his energies on science until he prepared to come to the United States at the age of twenty-eight.

Nikola Tesla as a young man

Working for Edison

8   Tesla started out working for Thomas Edison when he immigrated to the United States in 1884. Edison had developed direct current (DC) transmission—a way of sending electricity over long distances to power his famous lightbulb. But DC power was not efficient. It needed power stations every two miles. It required vast amounts of copper wiring. Edison offered Tesla $50,000 if he could improve the way energy was transmitted. But after Tesla presented his improvements to Edison, Edison said that he had been joking about the $50,000. Furious, Tesla quit. The two became competitors.

Edison's lab in New Jersey where Tesla first worked

The Amazing Alternating Current

9   Tesla kept working on his own idea of how to improve the way energy was transmitted. Finally, he came up with alternating current (AC) transmission. Instead of electricity going in one direction, it would move rapidly back and forth. This would allow it to carry higher levels of electricity

This is one of Tesla's early AC motors.

more efficiently over longer distances than DC transmission. He left Edison and built a small, efficient AC motor. A businessman named George Westinghouse saw AC's potential and bought Tesla's patent in 1885. Now Edison and Tesla were engaged in a battle of science—the war of the currents. The winner would lay claim as a visionary scientist and also reap millions of dollars in business. Neither wanted to lose, but which power would ultimately win?

Masses of electrical and telegraph wires fell down during New York's disastrous Blizzard of 1888. People were killed. Edison's heavy copper wiring and DC system were blamed.

Tesla demonstrates wireless transmission of power
and energy during an 1891 lecture.

The War of Currents

10   Over the next few years, the battle raged on
between Edison on one side and Westinghouse
and Tesla on the other. Edison tried to persuade
people that AC current was too dangerous.
Westinghouse later said this about Edison and
his campaign:

11   *I remember Tom [Edison] telling them that direct
current was like a river flowing peacefully to the
sea, while alternating current was like a torrent
rushing violently over a precipice . . . they even had
a professor named Harold Brown who went around
talking to audiences . . . and electrocuting dogs and
old horses—even an elephant—right on stage, to
show how dangerous alternating current was.*

12   Tesla argued that DC current was too weak
and inefficient. Edison was a powerful opponent,
but so was Tesla. Well-dressed, elegant, and a true
showman, he loved giving demonstrations to get
people excited about his inventions. He wasn't
afraid to fight for what he believed in. And he
believed in AC transmission.

World's Fair

13   The battle finally came to a head when Edison and Westinghouse, using Tesla's ideas, competed for the chance to provide electricity for the

The Chicago World's Fair—the final battle in the War of Currents

lights of the Chicago World's Fair in 1893. Edison said he would light the fair for one million dollars. Westinghouse said he could light the fair for half that amount. The two sides set up rival systems. But when they were turned on, Edison's lights looked dim compared with Tesla's. AC power won the battle. This current is used in the United States today.

Harnessing the Power of Niagara Falls

14   But Tesla wasn't done. From 1893 to 1896, he worked on a massive project to harness the power of Niagara Falls for electricity. Tesla's investors were nervous, but when a switch was flipped on, electricity flowed to the city of Buffalo, miles away. Tesla had created the first successful hydroelectric project.

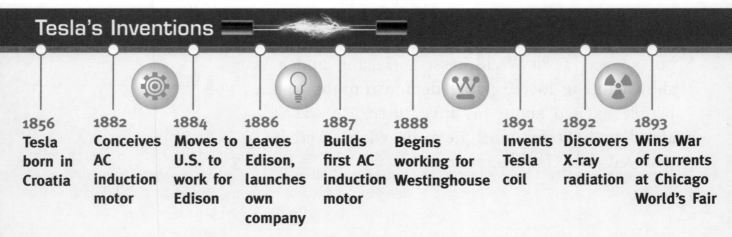

Tesla's Inventions

1856 Tesla born in Croatia

1882 Conceives AC induction motor

1884 Moves to U.S. to work for Edison

1886 Leaves Edison, launches own company

1887 Builds first AC induction motor

1888 Begins working for Westinghouse

1891 Invents Tesla coil

1892 Discovers X-ray radiation

1893 Wins War of Currents at Chicago World's Fair

Tesla Coil

15   In 1891, Tesla invented the Tesla coil. This device uses electricity from devices such as radios and televisions. It then transforms it into very high voltage. A large coil can light up fluorescent lights up to fifty feet away. Larger Tesla coils can emit, or produce, bolts of lightning and sparks of electricity. Today, many science museums have massive Tesla coils that demonstrate that power.

Tesla Fades from History

16   In later years, Tesla had fewer successful inventions. By the time he died in 1943, Tesla had mostly faded from public memory. Today, there is a movement to restore Tesla to the prominent place he deserves for his work in science. The Nikola Tesla museum in Belgrade, Serbia, showcases Tesla's achievements. The California-based electric car company, Tesla Motors, is named after him. The unit of magnetic flux density called Tesla is named for him as well. The Tesla unit measures the concentration of a magnetic field. Tesla received this high honor from the international scientific community in recognition of his work and many inventions. Tesla made the world a brighter place in his lifetime and his influence continues today.

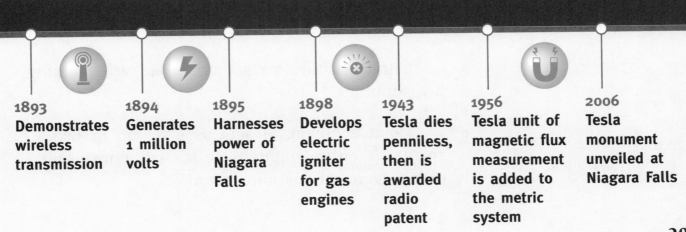

1893 Demonstrates wireless transmission

1894 Generates 1 million volts

1895 Harnesses power of Niagara Falls

1898 Develops electric igniter for gas engines

1943 Tesla dies penniless, then is awarded radio patent

1956 Tesla unit of magnetic flux measurement is added to the metric system

2006 Tesla monument unveiled at Niagara Falls

Remember to annotate as you read.

Notes

A Night in Tesla's Lab

1   Last night I dreamed that I visited Nikola Tesla in his laboratory. Why did I dream of this great scientist and inventor? Maybe it's because I'm reading about Tesla in school, or maybe it's because his inventions fascinate me!

2   In my dream, Tesla and I were friends. As we talked in his lab, Tesla reminisced about his mother, who invented household appliances. He described how he had emigrated from Europe to America with just four cents in his pocket. Then he showed me some of his inventions.

3   Tesla enjoyed having an audience, and his laboratory was the perfect venue for a show. He demonstrated a coil that he had invented, and I audibly gasped as the coil generated a spectacular electrical display. Next Tesla showed me his early X-ray shadowgraphs and a radio-controlled boat that he had built. He laughingly admitted that people who didn't understand his work believed he controlled the boat with his mind.

4   Tesla's mood turned serious when he talked about the possibility of transmitting wireless energy and receiving signals from outer space. He confided to me that he was inventing a death beam that would make war impossible. I couldn't believe it! It's what we call a laser beam! I was about to ask Tesla more when I heard a voice.

5   "Chris, it's time to get up!" Dad was shaking my shoulder.

6   "What a dream," I said as I sat up in bed. "I spent the entire night in Tesla's laboratory and I didn't even get his autograph!"

BuildReflectWrite

Build Knowledge

Identify two of Thomas Edison's and Nikola Tesla's inventions. Then draw a conclusion about the importance of these inventions. Which one do you think had the most significant impact on society?

Invention	Edison	Tesla
Invention #1		
Invention #2		
Conclusion:		

Reflect

Where do scientific discoveries lead us?

Based on this week's texts, write down new ideas and questions you have about the essential question.

_____

_____

_____

_____

_____

_____

Research and Writing

Opinion

Research one invention or discovery that has affected the way we power our lives. In an opinion essay, explain why you think this invention or discovery has had the greatest impact on the way we use electricity. Make sure to defend your opinion with reasons and evidence.

Write Your Account

Use your research results to draft, revise, and edit your opinion essay. Share your opinion essay with your peers.

Support for Collaborative Conversation

Discussion Prompts

Express ideas or opinions . . .

When I read _____, it made me think that _____.

Based on the information in _____, my [opinion/idea] is _____.

As I [listened to/read/watched] _____, it occurred to me that _____.

It was important that _____.

Gain the floor . . .

I would like to add a comment. _____.

Excuse me for interrupting, but _____.

That made me think of _____.

Build on a peer's idea or opinion . . .

That's an interesting point. It makes me think _____.

If _____, then maybe _____.

[Name] said _____. That could mean that _____.

Express agreement with a peer's idea . . .

I agree that _____ because _____.

I also feel that _____ because _____.

[Name] made the comment that _____, and I think that is important because _____.

Respectfully express disagreement . . .

I understand your point of view that _____, but in my opinion _____ because _____.

That is an interesting idea, but did you consider the fact that _____?

I do not agree that _____. I think that _____ because _____.

Ask a clarifying question . . .

You said _____. Could you explain what you mean by that?

I don't understand how your evidence supports that inference. Can you say more?

I'm not sure I understand. Are you saying that _____?

Clarify for others . . .

When I said _____, what I meant was that _____.

I reached my conclusion because _____.

Group Roles

Discussion Director:
Your role is to guide the group's discussion and be sure that everyone has a chance to express his or her ideas.

Notetaker:
Your job is to record the group's ideas and important points of discussion.

Summarizer:
In this role, you will restate the group's comments and conclusions.

Presenter:
Your role is to provide an overview of the group's discussion to the class.

Timekeeper:
You will track the time and help to keep your peers on task.

Making Meaning with Words

Word	My Definition	My Sentence
account (p. 23)		
cease (p. 12)		
complex (p. 16)		
convert (p. 14)		
devoted (p. 23)		
estimated (p. 12)		
preserve (p. 12)		
restored (p. 4)		
suspended (p. 7)		
transmission (p. 17)		

Lexile 810L–1060L

Build Knowledge Across 10 Topic Strands

Government and Citizenship

Character

Life Science

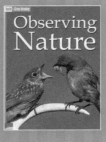

Point of View

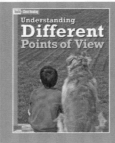

Technology and Society

Theme

History and Culture

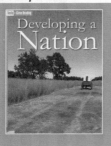

Earth Science

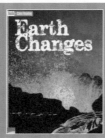

Economics

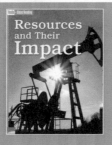

Physical Science

BENCHMARK EDUCATION COMPANY

Grade 4 • Unit 10

ISBN 978-1-4900-9206-5

9 781490 092065